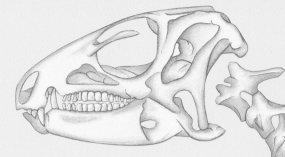

Awesome Dinosaurs

DUCKBILLS and BONEHEADS

Michael Benton

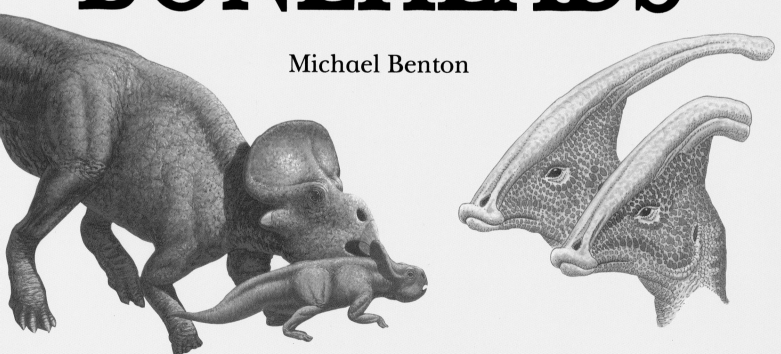

COPPER BEECH BOOKS
Brookfield, Connecticut

© Aladdin Books Ltd 2001

Produced by:
Aladdin Books Ltd
28 Percy Street
London W1P 0LD

ISBN 0–7613–2160–8

First published in the United States in 2001 by:
Copper Beech Books,
an imprint of
The Millbrook Press
2 Old New Milford Road
Brookfield,
Connecticut 06804

Editor:
Kathy Gemmell

Designers:
Flick, Book Design & Graphics
Simon Morse

Illustrators:
James Field, Ross Watton—SGA
Additional illustrations:
Sarah Smith—SGA
Cartoons: Jo Moore

Certain illustrations have appeared in earlier books created by Aladdin Books.

Printed in UAE
Cataloging-in-Publication data is on file at the Library of Congress.

Contents

Introduction

Find out for yourself all about horned dinosaurs, bonehead dinosaurs, and dinosaurs that had a bill like a duck's.

Dinosaurs lived on Earth millions and millions of years ago and were among the most successful animals of all time. Scientists called paleontologists are constantly unearthing amazing information and making exciting new discoveries about duckbilled, horned, and bonehead dinosaurs. They study their remains, called fossils, which have been preserved in ancient rocks.

Spot and count!

Q: Why watch out for these boxes?

A: They give answers to the dinosaur questions you always wanted to ask.

zoom in on...

Dinosaur bits

Look for these boxes to take a closer look at duckbill and bonehead features.

Awesome factS

Watch out for these diamonds to learn more about the truly weird and wonderful facts about duckbills, boneheads, and their world.

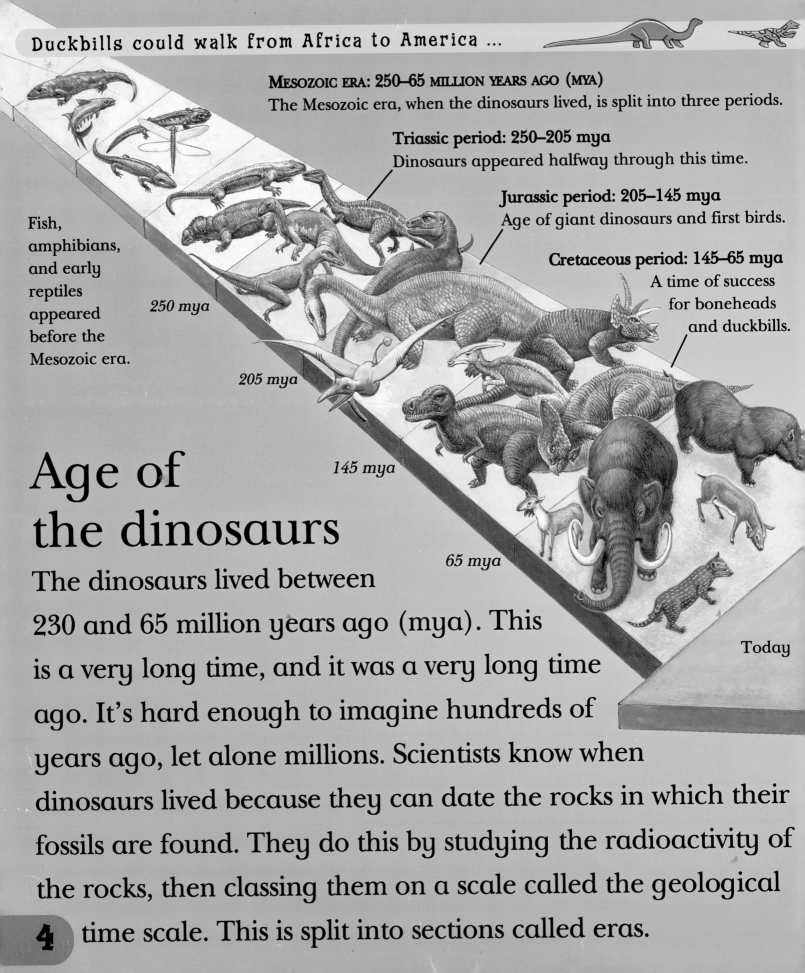

MESOZOIC ERA: 250–65 MILLION YEARS AGO (MYA)
The Mesozoic era, when the dinosaurs lived, is split into three periods.

Triassic period: 250–205 mya
Dinosaurs appeared halfway through this time.

Jurassic period: 205–145 mya
Age of giant dinosaurs and first birds.

Cretaceous period: 145–65 mya
A time of success
for boneheads
and duckbills.

Fish,
amphibians,
and early
reptiles
appeared
before the
Mesozoic era.

250 mya

205 mya

145 mya

65 mya

Today

Age of the dinosaurs

The dinosaurs lived between
230 and 65 million years ago (mya). This
is a very long time, and it was a very long time
ago. It's hard enough to imagine hundreds of
years ago, let alone millions. Scientists know when
dinosaurs lived because they can date the rocks in which their
fossils are found. They do this by studying the radioactivity of
the rocks, then classing them on a scale called the geological
time scale. This is split into sections called eras.

4

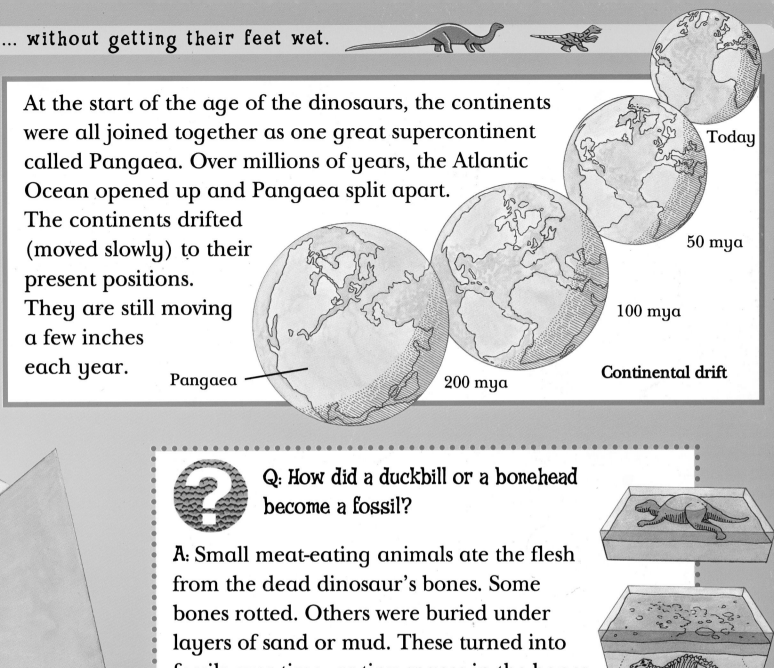

At the start of the age of the dinosaurs, the continents were all joined together as one great supercontinent called Pangaea. Over millions of years, the Atlantic Ocean opened up and Pangaea split apart. The continents drifted (moved slowly) to their present positions. They are still moving a few inches each year.

Today

50 mya

100 mya

200 mya

Pangaea

Continental drift

Q: How did a duckbill or a bonehead become a fossil?

A: Small meat-eating animals ate the flesh from the dead dinosaur's bones. Some bones rotted. Others were buried under layers of sand or mud. These turned into fossils over time, as tiny spaces in the bones filled with rock. Millions of years later, the fossilized bones are uncovered by water or wind action. Paleontologists dig the fossilized bones out of the rock and clean them, making sure they don't fall apart. They make maps and take photographs at the dig site so that they can tell later exactly where everything was found.

5

Horns, bones, and bills

Duckbills and their relatives were part of the group of two-legged, plant-eating dinosaurs called ornithopods. The bonehead group, called marginocephalians, included the boneheads themselves, called pachycephalosaurs, and the horn faces, called ceratopsians.

Stegoceras

Duckbills and boneheads were key dinosaurs of the Cretaceous. In the Late Cretaceous of Canada, herds of the ornithopod *Lambeosaurus* lived alongside the ceratopsian *Styracosaurus* and the smaller pachycephalosaur *Stegoceras*. All the duckbills and boneheads were plant eaters.

Awesome facts

Duckbills and boneheads traveled in huge mixed herds like modern antelope and wildebeest—hundreds of skeletons have been found in some fossil beds.

Lambeosaurus

Styracosaurus

7

Corythosaurus

zoom in on...

Duckbill teeth

Duckbills had hundreds of teeth arranged in tight rows, all designed for chopping tough plants. Some had as many as 2,000 teeth in total.

One of the best-known duckbills, *Corythosaurus* of North America, had a crest shaped like half a plate on its head. It had small hooves on its fingers and toes, suggesting that it walked on all fours. However, *Corythosaurus* also used its hands for grabbing food.

8

Although hadrosaurs looked like ducks, and may have been able to swim, they spent most of their time running about on dry land. Their huge tails were used for balance. Thin rods of bone called ossified tendons ran along the side of the tail and over the hips. These helped to keep the tail stiff.

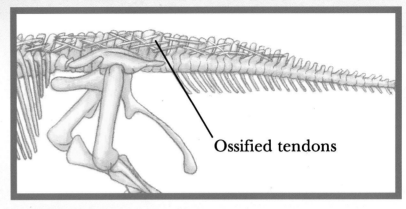

Ossified tendons

What makes a duckbill?

Duckbilled dinosaurs called hadrosaurs were the most successful dinosaurs of all. Hundreds of their skeletons have been found in Late Cretaceous rocks in China, North America, and Mongolia. Hadrosaurs had much the same body, but the heads were very different, often with bizarre crests.

Early ornithopods

The duckbills were common in the Late Cretaceous, but the ornithopod group had been around since the Triassic. The early ones were small and fast-moving, so they could escape from predators.

Lesothosaurus

Lesothosaurus had five fingers on its hand, just like a human. This shows that *Lesothosaurus* was a primitive form, since most later dinosaurs had only three or four fingers. *Lesothosaurus* used its strong little hands to gather leaves, and maybe even to carry them off if it was disturbed.

Q: What did *Lesothosaurus* eat?

A: Like all ornithopods, it ate plants. As it closed its jaws, its teeth rubbed firmly against each other. This shows that it could cut plant stems as if with a large pair of scissors.

Heterodontosaurus

Heterodontosaurus means "different-tooth lizard." It had long canine teeth, rather like a dog. These were not used for piercing flesh, but probably for grasping tough plant stems.

Canine teeth

Long-distance journeys

By the Late Jurassic, duckbills and their relatives lived worldwide. One famous one, *Dryosaurus*, was found in North America in 1894. A similar dinosaur was discovered in Tanzania in Africa in 1919. By 1970, it was realized they were identical.

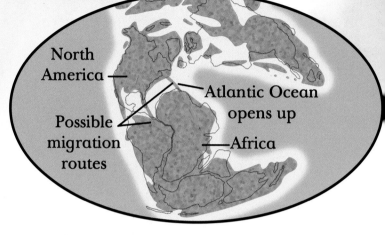

Middle Jurassic

North America —

Possible migration routes

Atlantic Ocean opens up

Africa

Identical dinosaurs across the world means long-distance migration. The Atlantic Ocean only began to open in the Middle Jurassic. Before then, *Dryosaurus* could easily have hiked from America to Africa on dry land.

Plant eaters often migrated huge distances in search of food. In hot, dry climates, they might have followed the wet seasons north and south to maintain a constant supply of leaves.

How many *Dryosaurus* can you spot?

Dinosaur dung

How do we know what dinosaurs like *Dryosaurus* ate? Fossils of dung, called coprolites, have been found, with chopped up leaves and stalks in them. Like horses, dinosaurs probably couldn't digest it all, so some came out in the dung.

zoom in on...

Dryosaurus had strong arms that it used to reach for leaves. Its jaws were lined with broad teeth, good for chopping up stems. But it had a special feature, seen in all the dinosaurs of the ornithopod group—a horny beak at the front of the jaws, which it used to cut and bite plants.

Dryosaurus

Iguanodon was named by Gideon Mantell in 1825. His wife, Mary Ann, had found some teeth in a pile of rubble beside a road in southern England. He later found more bones in a quarry nearby. The name means "iguana tooth," since Mantell thought its teeth were like those of the modern iguana lizard.

14

Naming the beast

Many skeletons of the ornithopod *Iguanodon* have been found in Early Cretaceous rocks in southern England, Belgium, France, and Germany. *Iguanodon* had a wicked thumb spike, which it may have used to defend itself.

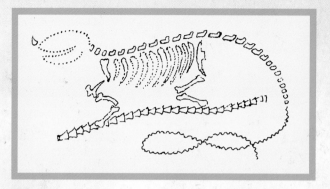

Early collectors only had a few bones of *Iguanodon,* and they thought a heavy, pointed bone was a nose horn (above). Only when whole skeletons were found in 1877 did they see that this bone was in fact the thumb spike.

Iguanodon

Awesome factS
From examination of fossil feet, paleontologists think that *Iguanodon* may have suffered from arthritis in its ankles.

How many runners are there?

Runners

Hypsilophodon was a small, fast-moving ornithopod. Great herds of them lived in southern England, and close relatives have been found all over the world. They were among the most successful dinosaurs of their day.

Hypsilophodon

Stride length

Length of leg

Dinosaur speeds can be calculated by looking at their leg skeletons and footprints. When an animal runs faster, it takes longer strides—just like you! If you know the stride length, measured from fossil tracks, and the length of the leg, then you can work out the speed.

Awesome facts

Hypsilophodon could run at a speed of twenty miles per hour or more, which is about the same speed as a racehorse.

Q: Did *Hypsilophodon* hide in trees?

A: Some old reconstructions show *Hypsilophodon* perching in a tree. This would have been impossible, however, because its feet would not have been able to grasp a branch.

Hypsilophodon certainly hid from predators in bushes and found food among the trees, but it was definitely not an oversized perching bird!

Parasaurolophus tooted like a clarinet.

Parasaurolophus

Parasaurolophus had one of the most amazing crests—a long tube on top of its head. This was once thought to be a snorkel that allowed the dinosaur to breathe underwater. But there is no hole at the end. It probably allowed one *Parasaurolophus* to identify another.

zoom in on...

Inside the crest

The breathing tubes in a crest ran up from the nostrils to the end of the crest, then back and down to the throat. When a hadrosaur breathed in or out, the air went all around this long set of tubes. This would have made a noise, since the tubes were like part of a trumpet.

Air

18

Crests and snorkels

The duckbills of the Late Cretaceous, the hadrosaurs, are famous for their amazing headgear—a huge range of crests, horns, and snorkel-like tubes. Scientists have debated what they were for. They may have marked out different species by their various shapes and sounds.

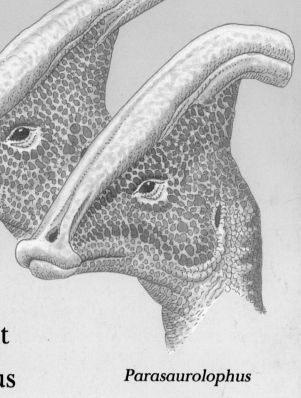

Parasaurolophus

Corythosaurus

Different crests made different noises. Each hadrosaur had its own special honk or toot. In a herd of many different species, hadrosaurs of different types could look and listen for their mates.

Males and females of a species also had different crest shapes, so they looked and sounded a bit different from each other. One of the *Parasaurolophus* had a shorter crest than the other, but scientists don't know whether the short-crested form was the male or the female.

Tsintaosaurus

19

Parents

Amazing discoveries have been made recently about how duckbills looked after their young. *Maiasaura* of North America cared for their little hatchlings and fed them softened plant fragments. *Maiasaura* means "good mother lizard."

Awesome facts

Maiasaura hatchlings were over three feet long before they left the nest. Until then, their moms brought them tender shoots and leaves to eat.

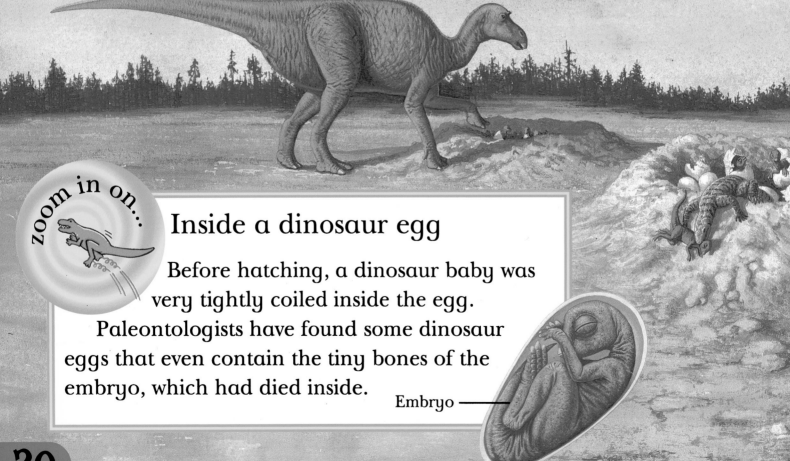

zoom in on...

Inside a dinosaur egg

Before hatching, a dinosaur baby was very tightly coiled inside the egg. Paleontologists have found some dinosaur eggs that even contain the tiny bones of the embryo, which had died inside.

Embryo ———

Maiasaura mothers dug nests in the ground as big as wading pools. They laid about twenty eggs and stayed around until they hatched. They fed the babies until they were big enough to venture out alone.

Q: Some birds nest in trees, so why didn't dinosaurs?

A: The dinosaur mom would first have had to find a strong tree, then she would have had to climb up somehow. Most dinosaurs were simply too big, or not nimble enough to manage this.

Spot the kidnapper!

The horn faces, called ceratopsians, probably head-butted each other. They may have sized each other up, trying to scare their rival away by looking fierce. They roared and may even have changed the color of the bony frill around their neck. If that didn't work, they might then crash heads and tussle.

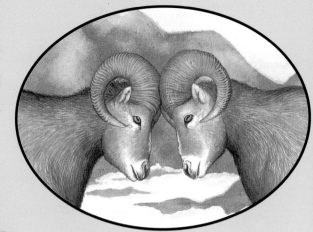

Styracosaurus

Just like boneheads, modern mountain goats crash heads together to see who is strongest in fights for territory or mates.

Pachycephalosaurs arose in the Early Cretaceous, but they are best known from the Late Cretaceous of North America and central Asia. They ran around on two legs, and they were all plant eaters.

Smackers

The boneheads called pachycephalosaurs ("thick-head lizards") are famous for having very thick skull roofs. The males may have had head-butting fights, just like some modern animals.

zoom in on...

Domeheads

There were two groups of pachycephalosaurs—one set with very thick, domed skull roofs, the other with lower, flatter skull roofs.

Stegoceras

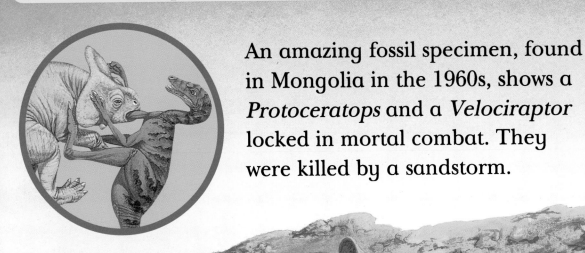

An amazing fossil specimen, found in Mongolia in the 1960s, shows a *Protoceratops* and a *Velociraptor* locked in mortal combat. They were killed by a sandstorm.

How many babies are there?

Protoceratops

Awesome factS

The first Mongolian dinosaurs were named in the 1920s, when expeditions set off into remote northern regions. Now, many amazing dinosaurs are known from there.

Young and old

Skeletons of baby dinosaurs show they were like human babies—big heads, big eyes, short legs, and knobby knees. One of the best series of family fossils found is of the ceratopsian *Protoceratops,* from the Late Cretaceous.

An amazing set of fossil tracks from North America shows how a herd protected its young. The tiny footprints of the babies are in the middle, with the bigger moms' and dads' footprints on the outside.

Fossil specimens from Mongolia include dozens of skulls of whole families of *Protoceratops.* Of course, the dinosaur became bigger as it grew older, but the shape of the skull also changed. The babies had huge eyes, short beaks, and weak jaws.

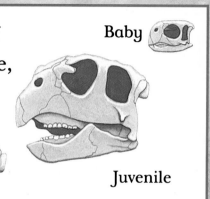

Baby

Juvenile

Adult

Family protection

Sometimes there is safety in numbers. When a meat eater threatened, many plant eaters could use the herd as a way to protect themselves. Like musk oxen today, ceratopsians may have formed a ring, horned heads outward.

Einosaurus

Albertosaurus

Styracosaurus

Even on their own, the ceratopsians were able to look after themselves. *Albertosaurus* had to be careful when it was faced by the long nose horn and spiky frill of *Styracosaurus*.

26

Einosaurus babies would stay in the middle of the group when the herd was under attack. The adults would present a united front, with their impressive horns facing the predator.

Ceratopsians had all kinds of face horns, some on the nose, others over the eyes. The neck frill also varied in size and decoration.

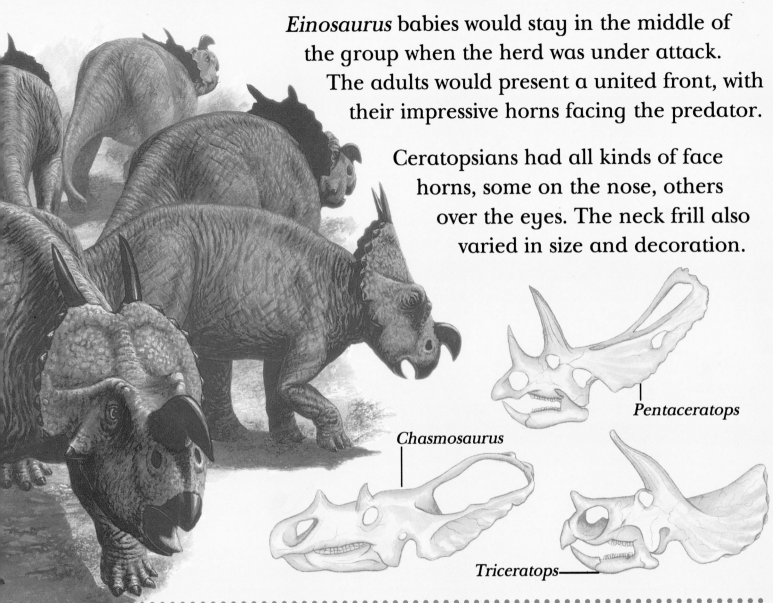

Pentaceratops

Chasmosaurus

Triceratops

Q: How fast could a horn face run?

A: Ceratopsians were built to move quite fast. It's likely they could trot, and even get up to twelve miles per hour. They weighed about five tons—the same as a modern elephant—and could move much faster than the giant plant-eating dinosaurs.

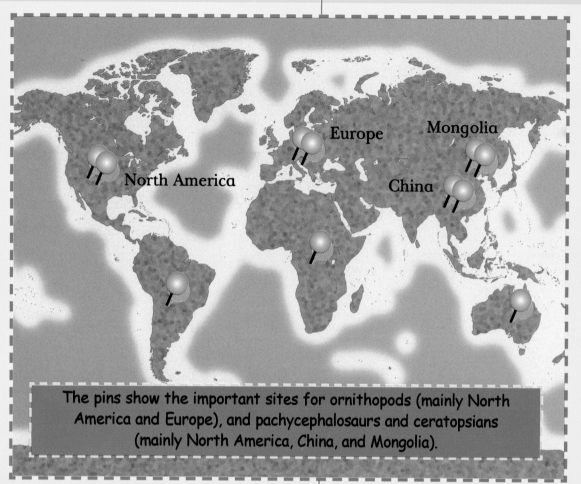

Europe
Mongolia
North America
China

Which
ornithopod
had long
canine teeth
like a dog?

Dryosaurus

The pins show the important sites for ornithopods (mainly North America and Europe), and pachycephalosaurs and ceratopsians (mainly North America, China, and Mongolia).

250 mya
(million years ago)

TRIASSIC

205 mya

JURASSIC

Which two
ornithopods on
these pages
lived millions
of years before
the rest?

Lesothosaurus

Heterodontosaurus

Duckbill and bonehead world

Ornithopods peaked in the Cretaceous, from *Iguanodon* to the later duckbills. The boneheads (pachycephalosaurs) and horned ceratopsians are only really known from the Late Cretaceous.

Einosaurus

Lambeosaurus

Hypsilophodon

Corythosaurus

Stegoceras

Styracosaurus

CRETACEOUS

Protoceratops

Iguanodon

Maiasaura

Parasaurolophus

29

SAURISCHIA

THEROPODA

SAUROPODOMORPHA

THYREOPHORA

ORNITHISCHIA

MARGINOCEPHALIA

ORNITHOPODA

30

Dinosaur groups

There were five main groups
of dinosaur: two-legged plant eaters such
as duckbills, called ornithopods; bonehead
and horned dinosaurs, called marginocephalians;
armored plant eaters, called thyreophorans; meat
eaters, called theropods; and big, long-necked
plant eaters, called sauropodomorphs.

● *Corythosaurus*

● *Diplodocus*

● *Sauropelta*

● *Einosaurus*

Tyrannosaurus rex ●

All dinosaurs are classed into one
of two subgroups, the Saurischia
and the Ornithischia, according to
the arrangement of their three hip
bones. The Saurischia, or "lizard
hips," had the three hip bones all
pointing in different directions.
The Ornithischia, or "bird hips,"
had both of the lower hip bones
running backward.

Hypsilophodon
(Ornithischia)

Carnotaurus
(Saurischia)

Glossary

Amphibian

A backboned animal that lives both in water and on land, such as a frog.

Ceratopsian

A plant-eating dinosaur with a bony frill at the back of its neck and horns on its face.

Continental drift

The movement of the continents over time.

Coprolite

A fossilized poop.

Cretaceous

The geological period that lasted from 145 to 65 million years ago.

Duckbill

An ornithopod dinosaur of the late Cretaceous, with a ducklike snout. Duckbills are sometimes called hadrosaurs.

Fossil

The remains of any ancient plant or animal, usually preserved in rock.

Geological

To do with the study of rocks.

Hadrosaur

Another name for a duckbill.

Jurassic

The geological period that lasted from 205 to 145 million years ago.

Marginocephalian

A plant-eating dinosaur with armored margins (borders) on its skull, like a ceratopsian or a pachycephalosaur.

Mesozoic

The geological era that lasted from 250 to 65 million years ago—the "age of dinosaurs."

Ornithopod

A two-legged plant eater from the ornithischian group, such as a duckbill.

Pachycephalosaur

A plant-eating dinosaur with a

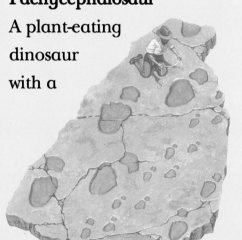

hugely thickened skull roof.

Paleontologist

A person who studies fossils.

Predator

A meat eater—an animal that hunts others for food.

Radioactivity

"Rays" of chemical energy that are given off at fixed rates. Measuring radioactive elements in ancient rocks allows geologists to calculate the age of the rocks.

Reptile

A backboned animal with scales, such as a dinosaur or a lizard. Most reptiles lay eggs and live on land.

Species

One particular kind of plant or animal, such as *Iguanodon*, the panda, or human beings.

Triassic

The geological period that lasted from 250 to 205 million years ago.

31

Index